GRIMORIUM

CW00922341

THE TRUE GR

First Edition 18th Century

New Edition 2018
Edited by Tarl Warwick

COPYRIGHT AND DISCLAIMER

FOREWORD

The Grimorium Verum is one of the most talked about texts within the occult, specifically because, like the infamous *Red Dragon,* its content unashamedly covers black rites which generally are either forsaken or couched in overtly christianized language in other similar works. We need look no further than much of the Solomonic Cycle materials such as the Book of Honorius or the Arbatel to see that this is the case. This work, though, does not mince its words, despite being misattributed and generally misunderstood by those reading it.

Like certain other works it claims a far older date than it has been reliably shown to originate from; namely the early 16th century, written in Egypt, although its manufacture is actually of the 1700s and of European manufacture. I speculate that its author was not an individual but rather that it was the work of a similar collective which much have designed the Red Dragon; in both cases early copies are in French and Italian, the material is somewhat similar in form, and in both cases there appear to be underlying steganographic qualities. I cannot verify this (much as no scholar can verify this sort of claim without knowing the specific, absolute origin) but it is at least sensible to theorize.

When we look to materials coming out of the enlightenment; the period of the very dusk of the 17th century into roughly the early pre-antebellum period, we see the same thing that actual Renaissance texts showcase in the same manner for similar reasons; the attribution of such texts to an older date and to a then already old occult pedigree; we might think of the Hermetic materials and their fixation on the near ancient *Hermes Trismegistus* despite their generally Renaissance era manufacture. In the modern sense we may not necessarily care that the date and authorship is in question (because the works are old regardless; most grimoires especially pre-date the American Civil War)- but those writing them at the time certainly cared; because the enlightenment era schools were philosophical, and their views at the time fancied by many but perhaps trusted by few, much as their Renaissance forebears alluded to antiquity in the same manner.

Within the Grimorium Verum (which, strangely, has also been released under the name *Grimoirium Verum* with an extra "i" for no apparent purpose) is contained what we might see as the same style of fusion occultism present in some of the titles competing for the moniker "grand grimoire" including the aforementioned Red Dragon. Here, folk magick, as it may be termed; simple invocations, spells, and quasi-alchemical rites involving herbs, stones, and so forth, are combined, and used for more materialistic goals than the Renaissance magicians were performing; to acquire love, or destroy someone who stole the turnips, or something of that nature. Here, as with other works, the folk magick is combined with elaborate ritualism more along the lines of Kabbalah or the works of the Gnostics. When we refer to *ceremonial magick* all of this material is more or less under one umbrella, and the early modern period of occultism with its fixation on the same (any world wars or cold war era occult path appears to share this trait) has done itself perhaps a disservice by conflating these materials together without ever bothering to notice the steganography present. Again with the comparisons to the Red Dragon! For both list the continents then of import separately in the early colonial fashion of the true time period of manufacture; Europe, Asia, Africa, and the Americas, generally being partitioned and differentiated on an absolute spiritual basis as under the control (here at least) of different forces which reign demonically over them.

I believe that this particular work, in one of its forms, was probably as well an influence upon the modern text released under the name "Necronomicon" and loosely based on the works of HP Lovecraft; I speak here of the "Simon" Necronomicon, rather than any of a number of pop culture influenced offshoots- for only this one version contains any authentic allusions to occultism whatsoever. Think what you wish about its actual manufacture and content, but it does show some similarities in design and in the materials used within the context of the rituals mentioned.

The inclusion of one ritual involving the head of a dead man belies the black magick nature of the work; such practices are indeed explicitly shunned by most texts of older origin and where they are embraced generally date to the 18th or 19th centuries. Even the concept of the demonic pact, present here and in similar works, doesn't generally appear at all in Renaissance works. Some well meaning but perhaps less bibliophilia-afflicted occultists appear to have overlooked this, and repeatedly tacked materials from their own chosen path onto the Grimorium Verum in an attempt to either increase its length or to liken it to their own slightly biased views, without appreciating it for what it actually contains.

If we presume a post- early 17th century origin for this work, the steganography present appears to be in the representation of the demons in their geographic zones, especially Astaroth. Here he is the lord of the Americas; and the going philosophy of the time (courtesy of Michaelis and French philosophy of the prior era) lists this specific being as concerned with rationalism and what we may loosely term secularity. When we consider the social movements present in the time period within the Americas, this seems to be a statement about militancy and social consciousness more than an explicit spiritual one. Beelzebub (or Beelzebuth, among other names), the lord of the flies, as it were, reigns over Africa. When one considers the generally gluttonous nature of the being we might say the author(s) of the text were again making a social statement. Lucifer, in Europe and Asia (likely referring to the near east, what was then Ottoman land, and not to, say, Japan or the far east, which would have been termed "the orient" in this time period) is of course, in the esoteric sense, the lord of light and illumination, the source from which these other powers flows, at times, or may be here considered its own equal and separate entity.

These philosophical considerations, of course, do not in any way detract from the text itself which is exceedingly do-it-yourself unlike certain magickal traditions which are essentially observations regarding, variously, language and numbers (as the Kabbalistic writings of late antiquity generally do) or natural science (as the Hermetic texts) or philosophy and creation studies as we may term it (courtesy of the Gnostics.) It is thus squarely in line with the enlightenment era cycle of works and reworkings, with all improperly attributed materials transmogrified in accordance with the philosophy of that same 18th century era. As with many similar works the description of the effects of rituals performed has a strange tendency to dwell on the minutiae of the workings; in the second book thus we get not a ritual to make a man or woman appear and entertain the occultist but rather a strange situation in which three men or women (according to the desire of the "conjurer") come, and subsequently dine, after which they draw lots to decide which of the three will entertain the conjurer further. It additionally dwells on literal and physical sacrificial ritualism involving the slaughter of animals which as far as my studies can tell appears nowhere in Renaissance workings. This work appears in as original a form as possible, although the language has been updated such that a modern audience is able to understand it without the use of archaic English, and obscure terms (such as the term "orision" for "prayer.) Otherwise it is original and intact.

CONTENTS

BOOK 3 (cont.)

BOOK 4

AD LECTORUM

In the first part of this work is contained various dispositions of characters, by which powers the spirits, or demons, are invoked, to make them come when you wish, according to their power, and to bring what is asked. Without any discomfort as well, for this provides also that they are content, for this sort of being does not give anything for nothing. In the first part is taught the means of calling forth the elemental spirits; of the Air, Earth, Water, and Fire, according to their affinities.

In the second part are expressed certain secrets, both natural and cosmic, which operate by the power of these same spirits. You will find the manner to make use of them, and all without any deceit.

In the third part is the Key of the work, with the manner of using it. Before starting this, it is necessary to be instructed by the following precept. There are three powers in this world, which are Lucifer, Beelzebub, and Astaroth. You must engrave their characters in the correct manner and at the appropriate hours. All of this is of consequence, and nothing is to be forgotten by the operator.

GRIMORIUM VERUM

BOOK I

CONCERNING THE CHARACTERS OF THE DEMONS

You must carry the aforesaid character with you. If you are male, in the right pocket, and it is to be written in your own blood or that of a sea turtle. You must put at the two half circles the first letter of your name and surname. And if you wish more, you may draw the character on an emerald or ruby, for they have a sympathy for the spirits, especially those of the sun, who are the most knowledgeable and better than the others. If you are a female, carry the characters on the left side, between the breasts, like an amulet, and always observing as much as the other sex, to write or have engraved the character on the day and in the hour of Mars. Obey the spirits in this, that they obey you as well.

The spirits who are powerful and exalted, serve only their confidants and intimate friends, by the pact made or to be made according to certain characters at the will of Singmabuth or of his secretary Aabidandes, of whom we will give you information. This is the perfect acquaintance to call, conjure, and restrain, as you will see in the Key of this book, where you will be given a method of making pacts with these spirits.

OF THE NATURE OF PACTS

There are only two kinds of pacts; the implied and the explicit. You will know the one from the other if you read this little book. Know, though, that there are many kinds of spirits, some attractive and some not attractive.

It is when you make a pact with a spirit, and have to give the spirit something which belongs to you, that you must always be on your guard.

THE KINDS OF SPIRITS

In regards to spirits, there are the superior and the inferior. The names of the superior spirits are Lucifer, Beelzebub, and Astaroth. The inferiors of Lucifer are in Europe and Asia and obey him. Beelzebub lives in Africa, and Astaroth inhabits America.

Of these, each of them has two who order their subjects, all that which the emperor Satan has resolved to do in the world, and so forth.

THE VISIBLE APPEARANCE OF SPIRITS

Spirits do not always appear in the same shape. This is because they are not themselves of matter or form, and have to find a body to appear in, and one suitable to their intended manifestation and appearance.

Lucifer appears in the form and figure of a fair boy. When angered, he seems to turn a red color. There is nothing monstrous about him.

Beelzebub appears sometimes in monstrous form, sometimes like a gigantic cow, and at times like a male goat with a long tail. When angered he vomits fire.

Astaroth appears black, in human form.

Here follows the characters of Lucifer, Beelzebub, and Astaroth.

The character of Lucifer

The character of Beelzebub

The character of Astaroth

BOOK II

OF PLANETARY HOURS

Planetary hours can often be of great importance in performing various experiments. Failure to observe the proper day and hour may make the ritual impotent or cause unwanted effects. The astrological day is divided into twenty four hours, or sections, and begins and ends at sunrise with one of the two rulers ruling each hour. The week is seven days with a ruler ruling each day.

The seven days with rulers are as follows:

Saturday: Shabbathi (Saturn)
Thursday: Tzedek (Jupiter)
Tuesday: Madim (Mars)
Sunday: Shemeth (The sun)
Friday: Nogah (Venus)
Wednesday: Cohab (Mercury)
Monday: Lebanch (The moon)

There follows a chart of hours for the celestial bodies ruling the hours subjugated to the days of the week. The obvious pattern of the movements therein repeats and as such only seven hours need be given; hours 1,8,15,22 are identical, as are 2,9,16 and 23; 3,10,17 and 24; 4,11 and 18, 5,12 and 19, 6,13 and 20, 7,14 and 21.

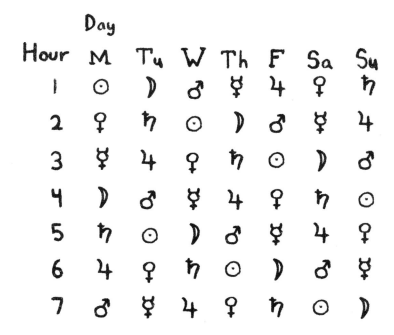

TO MAKE THREE MEN OR WOMEN APPEAR

It is necessary to be chaste for three days before these workings.

PREPARATION

On the fourth day, as soon as it is morning, clean and prepare your room, as soon as you have dressed yourself. You must be fasting during this process. Make sure that your room will not be disturbed for the whole of this fourth day. There should be nothing hanging, nor crossing the room, no tapestries or curtains or clothes hanging about the area, nor hats, bird cages, bed curtains, and such. Above all, make sure that everything is clean as much as possible.

CEREMONY

After you have eaten, go secretly to your room, which you have cleaned. Upon the table, set a white cloth and three chairs. In front of each chair, set a loaf of wheat bread and a glass of water. Now place a chair at your bedside and lay upon the bed, and say the following:

CONJURATION

"Besticitum confolatio veni ad me vertat Creon, Creon, Creon, cantor laudem omnipotentis et non commentur. Stat superior carta bient laudem omviestra principiem da montem et inimicos meos o prostantis vobis et mihi dantes que passium fieri sincisibus."

The three people, having arrived, will sit by the fire eating and drinking, and will thank you for having entertained them. If you are a man, three girls will come, but if you are a female, three young men will come.

Then the three will draw lots as to which will stay with you. If the operator is male, the girl who wins will sit in the chair which you have placed by your bedside and will stay with you until midnight. At this time she will leave with her companions, all without having been dismissed, the two others remaining by the fire while the third entertains you.

While she is with you, you may ask her any question about any art or science, or any other subject, and she will immediately give you her reply. You can ask where treasure is hidden, and she will tell you where it is and how it may be obtained. If the treasure is guarded by demonic forces, she and her companions will accompany you and guard you against them.

When she leaves she will give you a ring. If you wear this on your finger you will be fortunate while gambling. If you place the ring on the finger or any woman you will be immediately able to obtain what you wish from her. Your window, it should be noted, is to be left open during this process. You may perform this experiment as often as you wish.

TO MAKE A GIRL COME TO YOU, HOWEVER MODEST SHE MAY BE

Experiment with this marvelous power of the superior intelligences. Watch for the crescent or waning moon, and when it is present, make sure that there is a star between the eleventh hour and midnight. Before beginning the process, do this; take a virgin parchment and write on it the name of the girl which you desire. You must hold in your mind the face of the woman which you desire. As with the rest of the experiments in this book you must only use a virgin parchment which you yourself have prepared in the hour and day which are prescribed. The following figure you must write upon the parchment.

On the other side of the parchment write MELCHIAEL, BARESCHAS. Then put the parchment on the ground, with the part where the name of the person is written facing downwards. Place your right foot upon the parchment and your left knee, bent, on the ground, kneeling.

Then look to the highest star in the sky, while in this position. In your right hand, you must hold a candle of white wax sufficiently long to burn for an hour. Then say the following conjuration.

THE CONJURATION

"I salute you and conjure you, Oh beautiful moon, Oh most beautiful star, Oh brilliant light which I have in my hand. By the light which I have in my hand. By the air that I breathe within me, by the Earth that I am touching: I conjure you. By the names of the spirit princes living in you. By the ineffable name ON, which created everything. By you, oh resplendent angel GABRIEL, with the planet Mercuty, prince Michael and Melchidael.

I conjure you again, by all the holy names of God, so that you may send down power to oppress, torture, and harass the body and soul and the five senses of N., the whole name is written here, so that she may come unto me. Let her then be tortured, made to suffer. Go then at once, Go MELCHIDAEL, BARESCHES, ZAZEL, FIRIEL, MALCHA, and all those who are with you. I conjure you by the great and living God to obey my will, and I, N. promise to satisfy you."

Note that within the preceding conjuration, the symbol "N." denotes first the name of the woman and secondly the name of the operator.

When this conjuration has been said thrice, burn the parchment with the candle. Take care to see that the parchment is utterly consumed. On the next day, take the parchment ashes, put them in your left shoe, and let them stay there until the person which you have called comes to seek you out. In the conjuration you must say the date that she is to come, and she will not be absent. All of this will come to be if you are careful in carrying out the steps and do not tarry in this work.

GRIMORIUM VERUM

DIVINATION VIA URIEL

To succeed in this operation, he who makes the experiment must do all things which are told herein. He is to choose a small room or place which for nine days or more has not been visited by any woman who is impure.

This place must be well cleaned and consecrated by means of consecration and aspersion. In the middle of the room there is to be a table covered with a white cloth. On this is a new glass vial full of spring water, brought shortly before the operation, with three small candles of virgin wax mixed with human fat, a piece of virgin parchment, and the quill of a raven suitable for writing with. Also an ink pot of fine clay full of fresh ink, and a small container of metal with materials to make a fire. You must also find a boy of nine or ten years of age who shall be well behaved and cleanly dressed. He should be intelligent and sensitive and in a state of purity. He should be near the table. A large new needle is taken and one of the three candles is mounted upon it, six inches behind the glass. The other two candles should be at the right and left of the glass, an equal distance away from it.

While you are doing this say *"Gabamiah, Adonay, Agla, Oh lord of powers, aid us!"* Place the parchment on the right of the glass and the pen and ink on its left. Before starting close the door and windows. Now stir the fire, and light the candles. Let the boy go to his knees, looking into the vial that he may see the visions therein. He should have his head bare and his hands joined. Now, the master orders the boy to stare into the vial, and speaking softly into his right ear, the operator says the following conjuration:

GRIMORIUM VERUM

THE CONJURATION

"Uriel, Seraph, Josata, Ablati, Agla, Caila. I beg and conjure you by the four words that God spoke with his mouth to his fervent Moses. Josta, Agla, Caila, Ablati. And by the name of the nine heavens in which you live and also by the virginity of this child who is before you, to appear at once, and visibly, to reveal that truth which I desire to know. And when this is done, I will discharge you in peace and benevolence, in the name of the most holy Adonay."

When this conjuration is finished, ask the child whether he can see anything in the vial. If he answers that he sees an angel or any other materialization, the master of the operation will say thus in a friendly tone:

"Blessed spirit, welcome. I conjure you again, in the name of the most holy Adonay, to reveal to me immediately whatever I may ask of you."

Then say to the spirit:

"If, for any reason, you do not wish what you say to be heard by any others, I conjure you to write the answer upon this parchment, between this time and tomorrow. Otherwise you may reveal it to me in my sleep."

If the spirit answers audibly, you must listen with respect. If he does not speak, after you have repeated the supplication three times, snuff the candles out and leave the room until the following day. Return the next morning and you will find the answer written on the parchment if it has not already been revealed to you in the night.

GRIMORIUM VERUM

DIVINATION BY THE EGG

The operation of the egg is to know what will happen to anyone who is present at such an experiment.

One takes the egg of a black hen, laid in the daytime, breaks it, and removes the germ from within. You must have a large glass, very thin and clear- fill this with clear water and into it put the egg germ.

The glass is placed in the mid day in summer, and the director of the operation will recite the prayers and conjurations of the day.

These prayers and conjurations are such as are found in the *Key of Solomon* in which we treat amply of the airy spirits. And with the index finger, agitate the water, to make the germ turn, Leave it to rest a moment, and then look at it through the glass, not touching it. Then you will see the answer, and it should be tried on a work day, because there are spirits which will come during the times of ordinary occupations.

If one wishes to see if a boy or a girl is a virgin, the germ will fall to the bottom. If he or she is not, it will be as usual.

A RARE AND SURPRISING MAGICAL SECRET

The manner of making the Mirror of Solomon, useful for all divination. In the name of the lord, amen, you shall see in this mirror anything which you may desire. In the name of the lord who is blessed, in the name of the lord, amen. First, you will abstain from all actions of the flesh, and also any sin whether in word or deed, during the period of time laid down herein.

22

Secondly, you must perform acts of good and piety. Third, take a plate of the finest steel, burnished and slightly curved, and with the blood of a white pigeon write upon it, at its corners, these names: JEHOVA, ELOYM, METATRON, ADONAY.

Place the steel in a clean white cloth. Look for the new moon, in the first hour after the sun has set, and when you see it as such, go to a window, look devoutly into the skies, and say:

"Oh eternal, oh king eternal, God ineffable. You who have created all things for the love of men, and by a concealed decision for the well being of man, deign now to look on me, N., who is your most unfit and unworthy servant, and look upon this, which is my intention.

Deign to send to me your angel, Anael, upon this same mirror; he does command and order his companions which you have formed, oh most powerful lord, who has always been, who is, and who will always be, so that in your name they may work and act with equity, giving me knowledge in everything that I will seek to know of them."

Now you are to throw down upon the burning embers a perfume. While you are doing this, say:

"In this and with this that I pour forth before your face, oh God, my God, you who are blessed, triune, and in the state of exaltation most sublime, who sits above the Cherubim and Seraphim, who will judge this Earth by fire, hear me."

This is to be said three times. When you have done so breathe three times on the mirror's surface, and say:

"Come, Anael, come, and let it be your agreement to be with me willingly. In the name of the father, the most powerful, in the name of the son, the most wise, in the name of the holy spirit, the most living.

Come, Anael, in the terrific name of Jehova. Come, Anael, by the power of the eternal Elohim. Come, by the right arm of the mighty Metatron.

Come to me, N., and order your subjects so that they may make known to me through their love, joy, and peace, the things that are hidden from my eyes."

When you have finished this, raise your eyes into the heavens and say:

"Oh most powerful lord, who causes all things to move in accordance with your will, listen to my prayer, and may my intentions be agreeable to you. Oh lord, if it is your will, deign to gaze upon this mirror and sanctify it, that your servant Anael may come with his companions to me, and be agreeable to me, N., your poor and humble servant. Oh God blessed and raised above all the spirits of the heavens, you who live and reign eternally, amen."

When this is done make the sign of the cross over yourself and also on the mirror on the first day, and also on the next forty five days. At the end of this time, the angel Anael will appear to you, in the form of a beautiful youth. He will greet you, and order his companions to obey you.

It does not always require as long as this to cause the angel to appear, however. He may come on the fourteenth day, but this will depend upon the degree of application and fervor of the operator.

When he comes, ask him whatever you desire, and also

beg him to come and do your will whenever you should call him.

When you want Anael to come again, after the first time, all you must do is perfume the mirror, and say these words: "Come, Anael, come, and let it be your agreement..." and the rest of this one prayer to Anael, as we have given you above, until the "amen."

TO MAKE ONESELF INVISIBLE

Collect seven black beans. Start the rite on a Wednesday before sunrise. Take the head of a dead man and put one of the black beans in his mouth, two in each of his eyes, and two in his ears. Then make upon his head the character of the spirit Morail which follows.

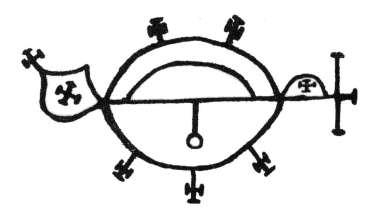

When you have done this, bury the head, with the face upwards, and for nine days before sunrise, water it each morning with brandy. On the eighth day you will find there the spirit mentioned to you, who will say "What do you desire?"

You will reply: "I am watering my plant." Then the spirit will say: "Give me the bottle, I desire to water it myself." In answer, refuse him this, even though he will ask again.

Then he will reach out with his hand and display to you that same figure which you have drawn upon the dead mans' head. Now you can be certain that it is the right spirit, the spirit of the head. There is a danger that another one might try to trick you, which would have evil consequences- and in that case the operation would not succeed.

Then you may give him the bottle and he will water the head and leave. On the next day when you return, you will find those beans which have begun germinating. Take them and put them in your mouth, and look at yourself in the mirror. If you can see nothing, it is well. Test the others in the same way, either in your own mouth or that of a child. Those which do not confer invisibility are to be reburied with the head.

BOOK 3

THE PREPARATION OF THE OPERATOR

When the implements are ready, the operator must prepare himself. This is first done by performing this preparatory prayer: "Lord god Adonai, who has formed man in your image, I, the unworthy and sinful, beseech you to sanctify this water, to benefit my body and soul, and cause me to be cleansed."

As he says this the operator is to wash his face and hands with the water that he is blessing.

This water is to be used for washing the hands and feet, it is necessary and most necessary, to abstain three days from sin and above all mortally, however much the human frailty may be, and especially guard your chastity.

During the three days, study the book and during this time, pray five times during the day and four times each night, with the following form:

"Astrachios, Aach, Acala, Abedumabal, Silat, Anabotes, Jesubilin, Scingin, Geneon, Domol. Oh lord my God, you who are seated higher than the heavens, you who see even unto the depths, I pray that you bestow unto me the things which I have in my mind, and that I may be successful in them. Through you, Oh great God, the eternal and who reigns forever and ever. Amen."

All this having been done correctly, all that remains is to follow your invocations and draw your characters and you do which follows.

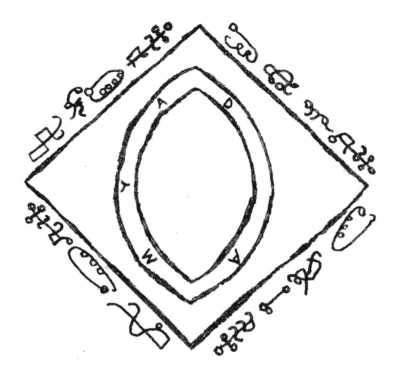

PRAYER: PREPARATION

"Yahweh, who has made man in your own image and resemblance out of nothing. I, poor sinner that I am, beg you to deign bless and sanctify this water, so that it may be healthy for my body and my soul, and that all foolishness should depart from it.

GRIMORIUM VERUM

Lord God, all powerful and ineffable, and who led your people out of the land of Egypt, and has enabled them to cross the Red Sea with dry feet. Accord me this, that I may be purified by this water of all my sins, so that I may appear innocent before you. Amen."

OF THE MAGICKAL KNIFE

It is necessary to have a knife or lancet, of new steel, made on the day and hour of Jupiter with the moon crescent. If it cannot be made, it may be purchased, but this must be done at the time, as above.

Having achieved this, you will say the prayer following, which will serve for the knife and lancet.

CONJURATION OF THE INSTRUMENT

"I conjure you, Oh form of the instrument, by the authority of our father God almighty, by the virtues of heaven and by the stars, by the virtue of the angels, and by the virtue of the elements, by the virtues of stones and herbs, and of snow, wind and thunder, that you now obtain all the necessary power for yourself for the perfecting of achievement of those things in which we are at present concerned. And this without deception, untruth, or anything of that nature whatsoever, by God the creator of the sun and angels. Amen."

Then we recite the seven psalms, and afterward the following words:

"Dalmaley, Lamekh, Cadat, Pancia, Velouf, Merroe, Lamideck, Caldurech, Anereton, Mitraton. Most pure angels be the guardians of these instruments, they are needed for many things."

THE SACRIFICIAL KNIFE

On a Tuesday at the new moon, make a knife of new steel which is strong enough to cut the neck of a young goat with one blow, and make a wooden handle on the same day and in the same hour, and with it you set down on the handle these characters.

Then asperse and fumigate it, and you have prepared an instrument for service when and where you wish.

THE MANNER OF ASPERSING AND FUMIGATION

First, there is the prayer which is needful on aspersion, and it is thus recited:

"Asperges me, domine, hyssopo, et mundabor; Lavabis me, et super nivem dealbabor. In the name of the immortal God. Asperge N. and clean you of all foolishness and deceit and you will be whiter than snow. Amen."

Then pour as the aspersion blessed water thereon, saying:

"In the name of the father, and of the son, and of the holy ghost. Amen."

These aspersions are necessary for every item of equipment, so also is the fumigation which follows. To fumigate, it is necessary to have a crucible, in which you place coal, newly kindled with a new fire, and let it be well ablaze. On this you place aromatics, and when perfuming the article in question, say the following:

"Angels of God, be our help, and may our work be accomplished by you. Zalay, Salmay, Dalmay, Angrecton, Ledrion, Amifor, Euchey, Or. Great angels, and do so also, Adonay, come and give to this a virtue so that this creature may gain a shape, and by this let our work be accomplished. In the name of the father, and of the son, and of the holy ghost. Amen."

Then recite the seven psalms, which come after, "Judicum tuum Regida" and "Laudate Dominum omnes gentes."

OF THE VIRGIN PARCHMENT

Virgin parchment can be made in many ways. Generally it is made of the skin of a goat or a lamb, or other animal which must be without blemish. After inscribing on the blade "AGLA" and having fumigated it, the knife will serve you for all purposes.

Remember that when you make the sacrifice in order to

obtain the virgin parchment from the lamb, all the instruments must be on the altar.

You make the magical staff of the art from Witch Hazel, that has never borne weight, and cut it with a single stroke on the day and the hour of Wednesday in the crescent moon. Engrave it with the needle, the pen, or the lancet, in the following characters; the seal and character of Frimost, to be inscribed on the first rod.

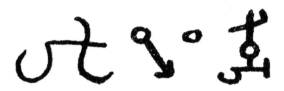

Then you make another staff of Witch Hazel, which has also never borne, and which is without seed. Cut it in the day and hour of Sunday, and on this you engrave the following:

The seal and character of Kleppoth is to be inscribed on the second rod. This having been done you say over the rod the following prayer:

"Most wise, most powerful Adonay, deign to bless, sanctify, and conserve this staff so that it may have the necessary virtue, oh most holy Adonay, to whom be honor and glory for all time. Amen."

OF THE LANCET

It is necessary to have a new lancet, conjured and prepared like the knife and sickle. Make it in the day and hour of Mercury, at the crescent moon. Now follows the method of sacrificing the goat.

MAKING THE SACRIFICE OF THE KID

Take your goat and place it on a flat surface, so that the throat is facing upwards, the better to cut it. Take your knife and cut the throat with a single stroke, while pronouncing the name of the spirit you wish to invoke.

For example, you shall say:

"I kill you in the name and in the honor of N."

This is to be well understood, and take care that you sever the throat at first, and do not require a second stroke, but see that it dies on the first.

Then you skin the goat with the knife and at the skinning, make this invocation which follows.

INVOCATION

"Adonay, Dalmay, Lauday, Tetragrammaton, Anereton,

and all you, holy angels of God, come and be here, and deign to infuse into this skin the power that it may be correctly conserved, so that all that is written upon it may become perfected."

After the skinning take well-ground salt and strew this on the skin, which you will have stretched out, and let the salt cover the skin well. Before you use the salt it must be consecrated using the benediction of the salt, which is given further in this book.

OF ASPERSIONS

You take an asperser with a bunch of mint, marjoram, and rosemary which is secured by a thread which has been made by a virgin maiden. The asperser is made in the day and hour of Mercury when the moon is at its crescent.

OF THE ASPERSION OF THE WATER

All water used in these experiments must be aspersed, by saying this over it:

"Lord God, father, all powerful, my refuge and my life. Help me, holy father, for I love you, God of Abraham, of Isaac, of Jacob, of the archangels and prophets, creator of all. In humility, and, calling on your holy name, I supplicate that you will agree to bless this water, so that it may sanctify our bodies and our souls, through you, msot holy Adonay, everlasting ruler. Amen."

The skin is allowed to dry after this, and before quitting the spot, say over the parchment:

GRIMORIUM VERUM

"Fe, Agla, Fod, Hoi, He, Emmanuel!" Stand guard over this parchment, in order that no spirit may take possession of it.

When the skin is dry it may be removed from its wooden frame, blessed and fumigated, and then it is ready for use. It is important that this must not be seen by any women, and more especially during their menstruation, or it will lose its power. The operator is to say one Mass of the Nativity then, and all the instruments must be placed upon the altar.

OF THE PERFUMES

These are to be aloe wood, incense, and mace. As for the mace, this is all that you need for the circle, and over the perfumes is to be said the following prayer:

THE PRAYER OF THE AROMATIC PERFUMES

"Deign, oh lord, to sanctify the creature of this, in order that it may be a remedy for the human race, and that it may be a remedy for our souls and bodies, through the invoking of your holy name. Agree that all beings which may breathe in the vapor of this may have health in their bodies and souls, through the lord who has fashioned the time eternal. Amen."

OF THE PEN OF THE ART

Take a new quill, and asperse and fumigate this in the same way as all other instruments, and when you are cutting its points, say the following:

"Ababaloy, Samoy, Escavor, Adonay. I have from this

quill driven out all illusions, so that it may hold within it with effectiveness the power needed for all those things which are used in the art for both the operations and the characters and conjurations. Amen."

OF THE INK HORN

You must purchase a new ink horn on the day and in the hour of Mercury. At this time also these characters are thus inscribed on it:

Then, newly made ink is exorcised with this exorcism before being placed in the horn:

"I exorcise you, creature of this ink, by the names Anston, Cerreton, Stimulator, Adonay, and by the name of he who created all by one word, and who can achieve all, so that you shall assist me in my work, and so this work may be accomplished by my desire, and brought to a successful end through agreement of God, he who rules all things, and through all things, omnipresent and eternal. Amen."

Then the ink must be blessed thus:

"Lord God, almighty, ruler over all and forever, you who causes to take place the greatest wonders in your creations, deign to grant the grace of your holy spirit through this ink. Bless it, and sanctify it, and impart to it a special power, that whatever we may say or do or desire may be accomplished, through you most holy prince Adonay. Amen."

GRIMORIUM VERUM

OF THE PENTACLE AND THE MANNER OF WORKING

I have put here the form of the Pentacle of Solomon, so that you may make the arrangements, they being of great importance.

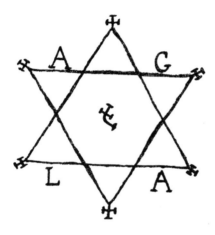

When you make your circle, before entering within it, it is to be perfumed with musk, amber, aloe, wood, and incense. And for the perfume which you will need for the invocations themselves, that is incense alone.

It is to be observed that you need to have always a fire during invocations, and when you perfume, this will be in the name of the spirit that you would invoke. When you are placing the perfume on the fire, say all the time:

"I burn this, N., in the name and to the honor of N."

It is to be remembered that you must hold the invocation

37

in the left hand, and in the right a rod of elder wood, and a ladle and a knife must be at your feet.

When all this is prepared, stand inside the circle. If you have companions with you, they are to hold their hands together. When inside, trace the form of the circle with the knife of the art. Then pick up the staffs, one after the other, reciting the fiftieth psalm. When the circle is complete, perfume and sprinkle it with holy water. Characters are to be written at the four corners of the circle. There are generally four pentacles, one at each point of the compass, and the spirit is prohibited from entering the precincts of the circle.

Then the invocations are to be repeated seven times. When the spirit appears, make him sign the character which you are holding in your hand, which promises that he will come whenever you call him. Ask for what you think is needed, and he will give it to you.

DISMISSAL OF THE SPIRIT

Let him go away with these words:

"Ite in pace ad loca vestra et pax sit inter vos redituri ad mecum vos invocavero, in nomine Patris et filii, et Spiritus Sancti, Amen."

GRIMORIUM VERUM

THE INVOCATION

HELOY + TAU + VARAF + PANTHON HOMNORCUM
ELEMIATH + SERUGEATH + AGLA + ON
TETRAGRAMMATON + CASILY

This invocation is to be made on virgin parchment, with the character of the demon upon it, which causes the intermediary spirit Scirlin to come. It is Scirlin that brings all others to you. For from this depend all others, and it can constrain them to appear in spite of themselves, as he has the power of Satan and is ready to serve him who gives a sacrifice, as it is said, that it is important that these beings be content on their own part or they will do you no service.

THE BENEDICTION OF THE SALT

"I exorcise you, oh creature of the salt, by the God who is living, the God of all Gods, the lord of all lords, that all fantasies may leave you, and that you may be suitable for the virgin parchment."

When this is finished let the skin with the salt upon it remain in the sun for a full day. Then obtain a glazed pottery jar, and write these characters around it with the pen of the art:

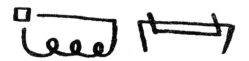

Obtain quicklime, and slake this with the exorcised

water, and put them in the jar. When it is a liquid place it in your goat skin and leave it long enough for the hairs to peel off of themselves.

As soon as the hair is in such a condition as to come off at a touch, remove it from the jar and peel the hairs off with a knife made of carved Witch Hazel. The knife must have had the following words said over it: "Oh holiest Adonay, put into this wood the power to cleanse the skin, through the holy name Agalon. Amen."

The skin, when peeled, may be stretched over a piece of new wood, and stones are to be placed on the skin, so that they hold it down. These are to be stones from a river bank. Before you place the stones it is important to recite the prayer of the stones over them, which is as follows.

THE PRAYER OF THE STONES

"Oh Adonay, most perfect and all powerful lord, allow that these stones may stretch the skin, and remove from them all wickedness, so that they may possess the required power. Amen."

GRIMORIUM VERUM

BOOK 4

Here begins the Sanctum Regnum, called the royalty of spirits, or the Little Key of Solomon, a most learned Hebraic necromancer and Rabbi. This book contains various combinations of characters whereby the powers can be invoked or brought forth whensoever you may wish, each according to his faculty.

INVOCATION TO SCIRLIN

In the day and hour of Mars, the moon being a crescent, and at the first hour of the day- which is a quarter of an hour before dawn- you will prepare a piece of virgin parchment, which will contain all the characters and the invocations of the spirits which you wish to produce.

For example, in the said day and hour, you will attach to the small finger of the hand (the pinky, the finger of Venus) a thread spun by a virgin girl, and pierce the finger with the lancet of the art, to get blood from it, with which you form your Scirlin character, as is given at the commencement of this book. Then write your invocation, which is that which follows:

HELON + TAUL +VARF + PAN + HEON
HOMONOREUM + CLEMIALH SERUGEATH
AGLA + TETRAGRAMMATON + CASOLY

You must write the first letter of your name where is the letter "A" in the sign of Scirlin and that of your surname where is the letter "D." The spirit Aglassis, whose character it is, is very potent to render you service, and will cause you to have power over the other spirits.

GRIMORIUM VERUM

Make above the character of the spirit that you desire to come, and burn incense in his honor. Then make the conjuration which is addressed to the spirit that you want to cause to appear, and burn incense in his honor.

CONJURATION FOR LUCIFER

"Lucifer, Ouyar, Chameron, Aliseon, Mandousin, Premy, Oriet, Naydrus, Esmony, Eparinesont, Estiot, Dumosson, Danochat, Casmiel, Hayras, Fabelloronthou, Sodirno, Peathan, Come Lucifer, Amen."

CONJURATION FOR BEELZEBUB

"Beelzebub, Lucifer, Madilon, Solymo, Saroy, Theu, Ameclo, Sagrael, Praredun, Adricanorom, Martino, Timo, Cameron, Phorsy, Metosite, Prumosy, Dumaso, Elivisa, Alphrois, Fubentroty, Come Beelzebub, Amen."

CONJURATION FOR ASTAROTH

"Astaroth, Ador, Cameso, Valuerituf, Mareso, Lodir, Cadomir, Aluiel, Calniso, Tely, Plorim, Viordy, Cureviorbas, Cameron, Vesturiel, Valnavij, Benez meus Calmiron, Noard, Nisa, Chenibranbo calevodium, Brazo tabrasol, Come Astaroth, Amen."

DESCENDING TO THE INFERIORS

Lucifer has two demons under him: Satanackia and

Agasisierap. Those of Beelzebub are Tarchimache and Fleurty. The characters of Satanackia and Fleurty are:

The two inferiors of Astaroth are Sagatana and Nesbiros. Their characters are:

There are yet other demons apart from these, who are under Duke Syrach. There are eighteen of these, and their names follow: Clauneck, Musisin, Bechaud, Frimost, Flepoth, Khil, Mersilde, Clisthert, Sirchade, Segal, Hicpath, Humots, Frucissiere, Guland, Surgat, Morail, Frutimiere, Huictiigaras.

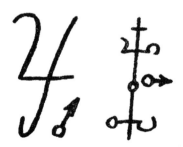

Bucon

Clisthert

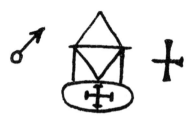

Frucissiere

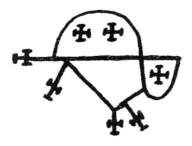

Guland

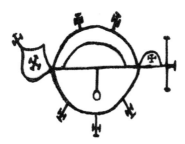

Morail

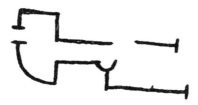

Hicpath

Frutimiere

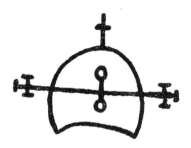

Huictiigaras

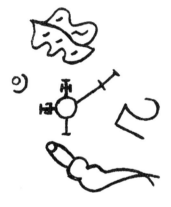

Humots

Khil

Mersilde

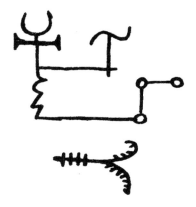

Musisin

Segal

Sirchade

Surgat

There are other demons but as they have no power we shall not speak of them. The powers of the eighteen mentioned above are thus:

Clauneck has power over riches, can cause treasures to be found. He can give great riches to he who makes a pace with him for he is much loved by Lucifer. It is he who causes wealth to be obtained.

GRIMORIUM VERUM

Musisin has power over great lords, teaches all that happens in the Republics and the affairs of the allies.

Bechaud has power over the forces of nature.

Frimost has power over women and girls and will help you obtain them as you wish.

Klepoth makes you see dreams and visions.

Khil controls earthquakes.

Mersilde has the power to transport anyone or anything at great speed.

Clisthert allows you to have day or night whenever you wish when you so desire.

Sirchade makes you see all manner of natural and supernatural animals.

Hicpacth will bring you a person instantly, though he be far away.

Humots will bring you any book you desire.

Segal will cause all manner of prodigies to appear.

Frucissiere revives the dead.

Guland causes illness.

Surgat opens all locks.

Morail can make anything invisible.

GRIMORIUM VERUM

Frutimiere prepares all manner of food for you.

Huictiigaras causes sleep in the case of some, and insomnia in others.

Under Satanachia and Sataniciae are forty five demons. Four of these are chief; Sergutthy, Heramael, Trimasael, and Sustugriel. The others are of no great importance. These spirits are of great advantage, and they work well and speedily, in the case that they are pleased with the operator.

Sergutthy has power over maidens and wives when things are favorable.

Heramael teaches the healing arts, including the complete knowledge of illness and cure. He also makes known the virtues of plants, where they are to be found, when to pluck them, and their making into medicine.

Trimasael teaches chemistry and all means of conjuring the nature of deceit or sleight of hand. He also teaches the secret of making the powder of protection, by means of which base metals may be turned to gold or silver.

Suftugriel teaches the art of magick. He gives familiar spirits that can be used for all purposes, and he also gives mandrakes.

Agalierept and Tarihimal are the rulers of Elelogap, who in turn governs matters connected with water.

Nebirots rules Hael and Surgulath. The former enables anyone to speak any language he wishes and also teaches the means whereby any type of letter may be written. He is also able to teach those things which are most secret and completely hidden.

Sergulath gives every means of speculation. In addition, he instructs as to the methods of breaking the ranks and strategy of opponents. Subject to these are the eight most powerful subordinates:

Proculo, who can cause a person to sleep for two days and nights with the knowledge of the spheres of sleep.

Haristum, who can cause anyone to pass through fire without being burned.

Brulefer, who causes a person to be beloved of women.

Pentagnony, who gives two benefits; of attaining invisibility and the love of great lords.

Aglasis, who can carry anyone or anything anywhere in the world.

Sidragosam, who can cause any girl to become nude.

Minoson, who is able to make anyone win at any game.

Bucon, who can cause hate and spite and jealousy between members of the opposite sex.

GRIMORIUM VERUM

CONJURATION FOR INFERIOR SPIRITS

OSURMY + DELMUSAN + ATALSLOYM + CHARUSIHOA
MELANY + LIAMINTHO + COLEHON + PARON
MADOIN + MERLOY + BULERATOR + DONMEDO
HONE + PELOYM + IBASIL + MEON + ALYMDRICTELS
PERSON + CRISOLSAY + LEMON SESSLE NIDAR HORIEL
PEUNT + HALMON + ASOPHIEL + ILNOSTREON
BANIEL + VERMIAS + SLEVOR + NOELMA
DORSAMOT + LHAVALA + OMOR + FRAMGAM
BELDOR + DRAGIN + Come, N.

DISMISSAL OF THE INFERIOR SPIRITS

"Ite in pace ad loca vestra et pax sit inter vos redituri ad mecum vos invocavero, in nomine Patris et filii et Spiritus Sancti. Amen."

Then you will burn the characters; because they will serve only once.

ANOTHER CONJURATION

"I conjure you, N., by the name of the great living God, sovereign creator of all things, that you appear in human form, fair and agreeable, without noise or inconvenience, to answer truthfully in all the interrogations that I will make. I conjure you to do this by the power of the holy and sacred names."

GRIMORIUM VERUM

PRAYER OF THE SALAMANDERS

"Immortal, eternal, ineffable and holy father of all things, who is carried by the revolving chariot unceasingly, of the worlds which continually revolve; dominator of the Ethereal places where is raised the throne of your power, above which your redoubtable eyes see all, and your holy ears hear all. Aid your children which you have loved since the birth of the centuries, for your golden and great and eternal majesty shines above the world, the sky, and the stars. You are elevated above all, oh sparkling fire, and you illuminate yourself by your own splendor, and there goes from your essence perfect rays of light which nourish your infinite spirit. That infinite spirit produces all things and makes the mighty treasure which cannot fail, to the creation which surrounds you due to the limitless forms of which she bears, and which you have filled up from the start. From this spirit comes also the origin of those most holy kings who are around your throne, tho compose your court, oh universal father.

Oh unique one, oh father of happy mortals and immortals. You have created in particular the powers which are marvelously like the eternal thought, and from your adorable essence. You have established them over the angels, you have created a third kind of sovereign in the elements. Our continual exercise is to worship your desires. We burn with the desire to possess you, oh father, oh mother, the most tender of mothers. Oh wonderful example of feeling and tenderness of mothers. Oh son the flower of all sons. Oh form of all forms. Soul, spirit, harmony, and name of all things, preserve us and we shall be blessed. Amen."

GRIMORIUM VERUM

DISMISSING ANY SPIRIT

When he has answered your questions and you are satisfied with him, you must send him away by saying thus:

"I thank you, Anael, for having appeared and having fulfilled by requests. You may therefore depart in peace, and shall return when I call to you."

TO SEE SPIRITS OF THE AIR

Take the brain of a roosteer, the powder from the grave of a dead man where it touches the coffin, walnut oil, and virgin wax. Make this into a mixture and wrap it in virgin parchment, on which is written the following:

GOMERT KAILOETH, with the symbol of Khil.

Burn it all, and you will see strange things. This experiment should only be done by those who fear nothing.

DISMISSAL OF THE SPIRIT

When you have written the conjuration on the virgin parchment, and have seen the spirit, being satisfied, you can dismiss him by saying the following:

"Ite in pace ad loca vestra et pax sit inter vos redituri ad mecum vos onvicavero, in nomine Patris et filii, et Spiritus Sancti. Amen."

THE END

Printed in Great Britain
by Amazon